Please return/renew this item
by the last date shown.
Books may also be renewed by
phone and Internet.

REVISED AND UPDATED

Transport Around the World

Emergency Vehicles

Chris Oxlade

Heinemann

www.heinemann.co.uk
Visit our website to find out more information about Heinemann Library books.

To order:
 Phone 44 (0) 1865 888066
Send a fax to 44 (0) 1865 314091
Visit the Heinemann Bookshop at www.heinemann.co.uk to browse our catalogue
and order online.

First published in Great Britain by Heinemann Library,
Halley Court, Jordan Hill, Oxford OX2 8EJ, part of Harcourt Education.
Heinemann is a registered trademark of Harcourt Education Ltd.

Editorial: Diyan Leake and Kristen Truhlar
Design: Kimberley R. Miracle and Ray Hendren
Picture research: Erica Martin
Production: Julie Carter

Originated by Chroma Graphics (Overseas) Pte Ltd
Printed and bound in China by South China Printing Co. Ltd

ISBN 978 0 4310 8697 2

12 11 10 09 08
10 9 8 7 6 5 4 3 2 1

British Library Cataloguing in Publication Data
Oxlade, Chris
Transport Around the World: Emergency Vehicles

A full catalogue record for this book is available from the British
Library

Acknowledgements
The publishers would like to thank the following for permission to
reproduce photographs: Alamy p. **10** (Jeff Greenberg); R.D. Battersby
p. **12**; Trevor Clifford pp. **22**, **28**; Corbis pp. **20**, **21**; Eye Ubiquitous p.
19; Getty Images/Photodisc p. **23**; Mary Evans Picture Library p. **9**; PA
Photos p. **27**; Photodisc p. **14**; Photoedit pp. **4** (Michael Newman), **15**
(A. Ramey); Quadrant pp. **16**, **17**, **26**, **29**; Royal Navy p. **18**; Science
Museum p. **8**; Shout Picture Library pp. **5**, **6**, **7**, **11**; Tony Stone Images
p. **13**; TRH Pictures pp. **24** (Canadair), **25** (Canadair).

Cover photograph of a South Korean police patrol car reproduced
with permission of Corbis/epa.

The publishers would like to thank Carrie Reiling for her assistance in
the publication of this book.

Every effort has been made to contact copyright holders of any material
reproduced in this book. Any omissions will be rectified in subsequent
printings if notice is given to the publishers.

Contents

Some words are shown in bold, **like this**. You can find out what they mean by looking in the glossary.

What is an emergency vehicle?

An emergency vehicle rushes to an accident to help **rescue** people. Cars, trucks, planes, and boats can all be emergency vehicles. They have special **equipment** that helps with the rescue.

These emergency vehicles are at the scene of an accident.

The crew of this fire engine are cutting open a car to rescue the driver.

Emergency vehicles have a **crew**. The crew drive the vehicle. They also work the special equipment to rescue people.

Special parts

This police officer is talking
to the control centre.

In the **cab** of an emergency vehicle there is a
two-way radio. Using the radio, the **crew** can
talk to a **control centre**. People at the control
centre tell the crew where the emergencies are.

Some emergency vehicles have bright floodlights that light up the scene of an emergency at night. They also have flashing lights and loud **sirens**. These let people know that the emergency vehicles are coming.

Different emergency vehicles come when there has been a big accident.

floodlights

Old emergency vehicles

The first fire engines could not carry much water. They were pulled along by horses. The **crew pumped** water to the fire by moving handles up and down.

This old fire engine was built in 1866.

Old lifeboats did not have **engines**. The crew had to row hard to get out to sea. In those days being in a lifeboat crew was a very dangerous job.

This kind of picture is called an engraving.
There were no photographs at the time
when this lifeboat was in use.

Where emergency vehicles are used

Police **patrol** cars, ambulances, and fire engines travel on roads. They often have to rush through busy traffic. The driver needs to be skilled and careful.

Police cars often have lights that flash to make sure that they can be clearly seen.

lights

Helicopters can rescue people in the mountains.

Some emergency vehicles such as helicopters fly through the air. They can reach places where there are no roads. Lifeboats travel on water to reach people who need help.

Police patrol cars

Police cars have clear markings so people can see them.

Police officers **patrol** the streets of towns and cities in patrol cars. Some patrol cars have powerful **engines** so that the officers can reach the accident quickly.

flashing light

Police car drivers need to stay in touch with other police officers and with the **control centre**.

The police officers hear about an emergency on their **two-way radio**. They switch on the patrol car's flashing lights and **sirens** so that other drivers can get out of the way.

Ambulances

An ambulance is a vehicle that carries ill or injured people to hospital. Inside the ambulance there is space to put a person on a **stretcher**.

An ambulance drives quickly through the streets to the hospital.

The ambulance crew have a driver and other people to treat the patient.

The ambulance **crew** drive the ambulance. They are also trained to do **first aid**. They treat the injured person on the way to hospital using first-aid **equipment**.

Flying doctors

In Australia, many people live in remote areas called the outback. Ambulances cannot reach them quickly. The Flying Doctor Service uses special planes that fly people to hospital.

A plane might be the best way to take a person to hospital.

On board the planes are beds for patients. There is also lots of **equipment**. The doctors can treat the patients as the plane flies along.

These doctors are getting ready to take a person to hospital.

Helicopters

rotor

This helicopter is about to make a rescue off a rocky shore where there are no roads.

Air–sea **rescue** helicopters help people who are in trouble at sea. A helicopter is lifted into the air by its spinning **rotor**.

18

A helicopter hovers over the scene of an accident. The pilot needs lots of skill to keep it still. People are lifted into the helicopter by a **winch**.

Lifeboats

Large accidents at sea might need many lifeboats like this one to save all the passengers.

A lifeboat is a boat that **rescues** people from sinking boats and ships. Lifeboats are fast and strong. They can go safely through enormous waves.

ramp

The ramp of a modern lifeboat helps it get quickly into the water.

A lifeboat must get to sea as quickly as possible when its **crew** get an emergency call. Lifeboats slide straight into the waves.

Fire engines

A fire engine is a vehicle that helps to put out fires. It carries lots of fire-fighting **equipment**. It has long ladders and water hoses.

There is equipment on a fire engine that tells the crew how much water there is to use and how hot a fire is.

Fire engines have to move water and equipment quickly to an emergency.

Some fire engines have a huge **tank** of water. They have a powerful water **pump**. Strong hoses can carry water from the pump or water pipe to the fire.

Water bombers

Sometimes there are big fires in forests. Special fire-fighting aircraft can drop water on to a forest fire. Normal fire engines could not get to the fire through the thick forest.

If the fire is too hot, the water can turn into steam, which is very dangerous.

There is a big water **tank** inside firefighting aircraft. The plane skims over a lake. Then the pilot scoops up water from the lake and fills the water tank.

The pilot of a water bomber has to be very skilled to scoop up the water and stay steady.

Airport fire engines

Every airport has its own fire engines. The engines are always ready to rush to the **rescue** in case a plane has an accident.

ท่าอากาศยานกรุงเทพ
BANGKOK INTERNATIONAL AIRPORT

Airport fire engines look very much like normal fire engines.

This fire engine is putting out the fire on a crashed plane.

spray gun

foam

An airport fire engine has a spray gun on the roof. The gun sprays thick foam like washing-up suds over a crashed plane. This stops the fire spreading.

Breakdown trucks

A breakdown truck goes to **rescue** cars, trucks, and buses that have broken down. A **mechanic** often uses the truck's tools to repair the broken vehicle.

This breakdown truck is large enough to rescue a broken truck or a bus.

ramp

This breakdown truck is taking away a car that has been in an accident.

If a vehicle cannot be repaired it is put on the back of the truck to be taken to a garage. A **winch** pulls the car up a ramp at the back of the truck.

Timeline

1800s   Fire engines are pulled by horses or firefighters. Their pumps are worked by people using their hands or feet.

1824   The world's first lifeboat service is started in the UK. It uses self-righting lifeboats that are rowed to sea by the **crew**.

1850s   The first ambulances are used during the Crimean War. They are horse-drawn carts with stretchers on top.

1885   The first proper car is built in Germany by Karl Benz. It has three wheels and is driven along by a petrol **engine**. Top speed is 13 kilometres (8 miles) per hour.

1928   In Australia, the Royal Flying Doctor Service is started. It carries doctors to remote towns in the Australian outback.

1940   The first successful helicopter makes a flight. It is the Sikorsky VS-300, designed by Igor Sikorsky.

1967   The Canadair CL-215 water bomber makes its first flight in Canada. It is designed to drop water on forest fires.

1990s   A system that allows emergency vehicles to change the traffic signal to a green light comes into use in the United States. This means that they can get to the emergency faster without waiting for a red light.

Glossary

cab — space at the front of a van or truck where the driver sits

control centre — base where there are people who tell emergency crew where the emergencies are

crew — group of people working together

engine — machine that powers movement using fuel

equipment — machines and supplies that help people do a job

first aid — helping someone who is injured, before they get to hospital

mechanic — person who repairs vehicles and their engines

patrol — travel around a town or city looking for emergencies

pump — machine that moves water

rescue — save from danger

rotor — blade on a helicopter that spins round

siren — device that makes a loud warning noise

stretcher — simple bed for ill or injured people that can be carried by two people

tank — large container for storing something, such as water

two-way radio — radio that lets you talk and listen to someone else

winch — machine like the reel on a fishing rod that pulls in a cable or rope with an engine or motor

Find Out More

Community Vehicles: Police Cars, Marcia S. Freeman (Capstone, 2006).

Emergency Vehicles, Seymour Simon (Chronicle, 2006).

Machines at Work: Rescue Helicopters, Cynthia Roberts (Child's World, 2007).

Machines at Work: Fire Trucks (DK Publishing, 2006).

Tonka Driving Force: Rescue Action, Craig Robert Carey (Scholastic, 2006).

Index